MY PRAYER REQUEST(INCLUDE THE DATE):

_____

_____

_____

_____

_____

_____

_____

_____

_____

_____

HOW & WHEN GOD RESPONDED TO MY PRAYER:

_____

_____

_____

_____

WHAT THIS EXPERIENCE TAUGHT ME ABOUT GOD:

_____

_____

_____

_____

"This is the confidence we have in approaching God: that if we ask anything according to His will, He hears us." - 1 John 5:14

MY PRAYER REQUEST(INCLUDE THE DATE):

_____
_____
_____
_____
_____
_____
_____
_____
_____

HOW & WHEN GOD RESPONDED TO MY PRAYER:

_____
_____
_____
_____

WHAT THIS EXPERIENCE TAUGHT ME ABOUT GOD:

_____
_____
_____
_____

"O my people, trust in Him at all times. Pour out your heart to Him, for God is our refuge." - Psalm 62:8

MY PRAYER REQUEST(INCLUDE THE DATE):

_____
_____
_____
_____
_____
_____
_____
_____
_____
_____

HOW & WHEN GOD RESPONDED TO MY PRAYER:

_____
_____
_____
_____

WHAT THIS EXPERIENCE TAUGHT ME ABOUT GOD:

_____
_____
_____
_____

"Jesus was telling them a parable about their need to pray continuously and not to be discouraged." - Luke 18:1

MY PRAYER REQUEST (INCLUDE THE DATE):

_____
_____
_____
_____
_____
_____
_____
_____
_____

HOW & WHEN GOD RESPONDED TO MY PRAYER:

_____
_____
_____
_____

WHAT THIS EXPERIENCE TAUGHT ME ABOUT GOD:

_____
_____
_____
_____

"And it is impossible to please God without faith. Anyone who wants to come to Him must believe that God exists and that He rewards those who sincerely seek Him."
- Hebrews 11:6

MY PRAYER REQUEST (INCLUDE THE DATE):

_____
_____
_____
_____
_____
_____
_____
_____
_____
_____

HOW & WHEN GOD RESPONDED TO MY PRAYER:

_____
_____
_____
_____

WHAT THIS EXPERIENCE TAUGHT ME ABOUT GOD:

_____
_____
_____
_____

"I call on you, my God, for You will answer me; turn Your ear to me and hear my prayer." - Psalm 17:6

MY PRAYER REQUEST (INCLUDE THE DATE):

_____
_____
_____
_____
_____
_____
_____
_____
_____

HOW & WHEN GOD RESPONDED TO MY PRAYER:

_____
_____
_____
_____

WHAT THIS EXPERIENCE TAUGHT ME ABOUT GOD:

_____
_____
_____
_____

"Pray continually." -1 Thessalonians 5:17

MY PRAYER REQUEST(INCLUDE THE DATE):

HOW & WHEN GOD RESPONDED TO MY PRAYER:

WHAT THIS EXPERIENCE TAUGHT ME ABOUT GOD:

"The LORD is my strength and my shield; my heart trusts in Him, and He helps me. My heart leaps for joy, and with my song I praise Him." - Psalm 28:7

MY PRAYER REQUEST (INCLUDE THE DATE):

HOW & WHEN GOD RESPONDED TO MY PRAYER:

WHAT THIS EXPERIENCE TAUGHT ME ABOUT GOD:

"For nothing will be impossible with God." - Luke 1:37

MY PRAYER REQUEST (INCLUDE THE DATE):

_____

_____

_____

_____

_____

_____

_____

_____

_____

_____

HOW & WHEN GOD RESPONDED TO MY PRAYER:

_____

_____

_____

_____

WHAT THIS EXPERIENCE TAUGHT ME ABOUT GOD:

_____

_____

_____

_____

"Continue steadfastly in prayer, being watchful in it with thanksgiving."
- Colossians 4:2

MY PRAYER REQUEST(INCLUDE THE DATE):

_____
_____
_____
_____
_____
_____
_____
_____
_____
_____

HOW & WHEN GOD RESPONDED TO MY PRAYER:

_____
_____
_____
_____

WHAT THIS EXPERIENCE TAUGHT ME ABOUT GOD:

_____
_____
_____
_____

"Our ancestors trusted in You, and You rescued them. They cried out to You and were saved. They trusted in You and were never disgraced." - Psalm 22:4-5

MY PRAYER REQUEST (INCLUDE THE DATE):

_____
_____
_____
_____
_____
_____
_____
_____
_____
_____

HOW & WHEN GOD RESPONDED TO MY PRAYER:

_____
_____
_____
_____

WHAT THIS EXPERIENCE TAUGHT ME ABOUT GOD:

_____
_____
_____
_____

"If you remain in me and my words remain in you, ask for whatever you want and it will be done for you." - John 15:7

MY PRAYER REQUEST(INCLUDE THE DATE):

_____
_____
_____
_____
_____
_____
_____
_____
_____
_____

HOW & WHEN GOD RESPONDED TO MY PRAYER:

_____
_____
_____
_____

WHAT THIS EXPERIENCE TAUGHT ME ABOUT GOD:

_____
_____
_____
_____

"He is near to those who call to him, who call to him with sincerity." - Psalm 145:18

MY PRAYER REQUEST (INCLUDE THE DATE):

HOW & WHEN GOD RESPONDED TO MY PRAYER:

WHAT THIS EXPERIENCE TAUGHT ME ABOUT GOD:

"When you call me and come and pray to me, I will listen to you. You will seek me and find me when you search for me with all your heart." - Jeremiah 29:12-13

MY PRAYER REQUEST (INCLUDE THE DATE):

_____
_____
_____
_____
_____
_____
_____
_____
_____
_____

HOW & WHEN GOD RESPONDED TO MY PRAYER:

_____
_____
_____
_____

WHAT THIS EXPERIENCE TAUGHT ME ABOUT GOD:

_____
_____
_____
_____

"For I cried out to him for help, praising him as I spoke. If I had not confessed the sin in my heart, the Lord would not have listened. But God did listen! He paid attention to my prayer. Praise God, who did not ignore my prayer or withdraw his unfailing love from me." - Psalm 66:17-20

MY PRAYER REQUEST (INCLUDE THE DATE):

___

___

___

___

___

___

___

___

___

___

HOW & WHEN GOD RESPONDED TO MY PRAYER:

___

___

___

___

WHAT THIS EXPERIENCE TAUGHT ME ABOUT GOD:

___

___

___

___

"Don't be anxious about anything; rather, bring up all of your requests to God in your prayers and petitions, along with giving thanks." - Philippians 4:6

MY PRAYER REQUEST (INCLUDE THE DATE):

___

HOW & WHEN GOD RESPONDED TO MY PRAYER:

___

WHAT THIS EXPERIENCE TAUGHT ME ABOUT GOD:

___

"Lord, in the morning you hear my voice. In the morning I lay it all out before you. Then I wait expectantly." - Psalm 5:3

MY PRAYER REQUEST(INCLUDE THE DATE):

_____
_____
_____
_____
_____
_____
_____
_____
_____
_____

HOW & WHEN GOD RESPONDED TO MY PRAYER:

_____
_____
_____
_____

WHAT THIS EXPERIENCE TAUGHT ME ABOUT GOD:

_____
_____
_____
_____

"So we fasted and prayed to our God for this, and he responded to us." - Ezra 8:23

MY PRAYER REQUEST(INCLUDE THE DATE):

_____
_____
_____
_____
_____
_____
_____
_____
_____
_____

HOW & WHEN GOD RESPONDED TO MY PRAYER:

_____
_____
_____
_____

WHAT THIS EXPERIENCE TAUGHT ME ABOUT GOD:

_____
_____
_____
_____

"And I tell you: Ask and you will receive. Seek and you will find. Knock and the door will be opened to you." - Luke 11:9

MY PRAYER REQUEST (INCLUDE THE DATE):

_____
_____
_____
_____
_____
_____
_____
_____
_____
_____

HOW & WHEN GOD RESPONDED TO MY PRAYER:

_____
_____
_____
_____

WHAT THIS EXPERIENCE TAUGHT ME ABOUT GOD:

_____
_____
_____
_____

"You will keep in perfect peace all who trust in You, all whose thoughts are fixed on You! Trust in the Lord always, for the Lord God is the eternal Rock." - Isaiah 26:3-4

MY PRAYER REQUEST(INCLUDE THE DATE):

_____
_____
_____
_____
_____
_____
_____
_____
_____
_____

HOW & WHEN GOD RESPONDED TO MY PRAYER:

_____
_____
_____
_____

WHAT THIS EXPERIENCE TAUGHT ME ABOUT GOD:

_____
_____
_____
_____

"The lions may grow weak and hungry, but those who seek the LORD lack no good thing." - Psalm 34:10

MY PRAYER REQUEST (INCLUDE THE DATE):

___

HOW & WHEN GOD RESPONDED TO MY PRAYER:

___

WHAT THIS EXPERIENCE TAUGHT ME ABOUT GOD:

___

"Let us then approach God's throne of grace with confidence, so that we may receive mercy and find grace to help us in our time of need." - Hebrews 4:16

MY PRAYER REQUEST (INCLUDE THE DATE):

___

HOW & WHEN GOD RESPONDED TO MY PRAYER:

___

WHAT THIS EXPERIENCE TAUGHT ME ABOUT GOD:

___

"If you ask Me for anything in My name, I will do it." - John 14:14

MY PRAYER REQUEST (INCLUDE THE DATE):

_____
_____
_____
_____
_____
_____
_____
_____
_____
_____

HOW & WHEN GOD RESPONDED TO MY PRAYER:

_____
_____
_____
_____

WHAT THIS EXPERIENCE TAUGHT ME ABOUT GOD:

_____
_____
_____
_____

*"Trust in the LORD with all your heart; do not depend on your own understanding.
Seek His will in all you do, and He will show you which path to take."*
- Proverbs 3:5-6

MY PRAYER REQUEST (INCLUDE THE DATE):

___

HOW & WHEN GOD RESPONDED TO MY PRAYER:

___

WHAT THIS EXPERIENCE TAUGHT ME ABOUT GOD:

___

"Give all your worries and cares to God, for He cares about you." - 1 Peter 5:7

MY PRAYER REQUEST(INCLUDE THE DATE):

HOW & WHEN GOD RESPONDED TO MY PRAYER:

WHAT THIS EXPERIENCE TAUGHT ME ABOUT GOD:

"I waited patiently for the LORD to help me, and He turned to me and heard my cry."
- Psalm 40:1

MY PRAYER REQUEST (INCLUDE THE DATE):

_____
_____
_____
_____
_____
_____
_____
_____
_____
_____

HOW & WHEN GOD RESPONDED TO MY PRAYER:

_____
_____
_____
_____

WHAT THIS EXPERIENCE TAUGHT ME ABOUT GOD:

_____
_____
_____
_____

"But blessed is the one who trusts in the LORD, whose confidence is in him."
- Jeremiah 17:7

MY PRAYER REQUEST (INCLUDE THE DATE):

_____
_____
_____
_____
_____
_____
_____
_____
_____
_____

HOW & WHEN GOD RESPONDED TO MY PRAYER:

_____
_____
_____
_____

WHAT THIS EXPERIENCE TAUGHT ME ABOUT GOD:

_____
_____
_____
_____

"Those who know your name trust in you, for you, O LORD, do not abandon those who search for you." - Psalm 9:10

MY PRAYER REQUEST (INCLUDE THE DATE):

_____
_____
_____
_____
_____
_____
_____
_____
_____

HOW & WHEN GOD RESPONDED TO MY PRAYER:

_____
_____
_____
_____

WHAT THIS EXPERIENCE TAUGHT ME ABOUT GOD:

_____
_____
_____
_____

"This is the confidence we have in approaching God: that if we ask anything according to His will, He hears us." - 1 John 5:14

MY PRAYER REQUEST (INCLUDE THE DATE):

_____

_____

_____

_____

_____

_____

_____

_____

_____

HOW & WHEN GOD RESPONDED TO MY PRAYER:

_____

_____

_____

_____

WHAT THIS EXPERIENCE TAUGHT ME ABOUT GOD:

_____

_____

_____

_____

"O my people, trust in Him at all times. Pour out your heart to Him, for God is our refuge." - Psalm 62:8

MY PRAYER REQUEST (INCLUDE THE DATE):

_____
_____
_____
_____
_____
_____
_____
_____
_____
_____

HOW & WHEN GOD RESPONDED TO MY PRAYER:

_____
_____
_____
_____

WHAT THIS EXPERIENCE TAUGHT ME ABOUT GOD:

_____
_____
_____
_____

"Jesus was telling them a parable about their need to pray continuously and not to be discouraged." - Luke 18:1

MY PRAYER REQUEST (INCLUDE THE DATE):

_____
_____
_____
_____
_____
_____
_____
_____
_____
_____

HOW & WHEN GOD RESPONDED TO MY PRAYER:

_____
_____
_____
_____

WHAT THIS EXPERIENCE TAUGHT ME ABOUT GOD:

_____
_____
_____
_____

"And it is impossible to please God without faith. Anyone who wants to come to Him must believe that God exists and that He rewards those who sincerely seek Him."
- Hebrews 11:6

MY PRAYER REQUEST (INCLUDE THE DATE):

_____
_____
_____
_____
_____
_____
_____
_____
_____
_____

HOW & WHEN GOD RESPONDED TO MY PRAYER:

_____
_____
_____
_____

WHAT THIS EXPERIENCE TAUGHT ME ABOUT GOD:

_____
_____
_____
_____

"I call on you, my God, for You will answer me; turn Your ear to me and hear my prayer." - Psalm 17:6

MY PRAYER REQUEST (INCLUDE THE DATE):

_____
_____
_____
_____
_____
_____
_____
_____
_____

HOW & WHEN GOD RESPONDED TO MY PRAYER:

_____
_____
_____
_____

WHAT THIS EXPERIENCE TAUGHT ME ABOUT GOD:

_____
_____
_____
_____

"Pray continually." -1 Thessalonians 5:17

MY PRAYER REQUEST (INCLUDE THE DATE):

_____
_____
_____
_____
_____
_____
_____
_____
_____
_____

HOW & WHEN GOD RESPONDED TO MY PRAYER:

_____
_____
_____
_____

WHAT THIS EXPERIENCE TAUGHT ME ABOUT GOD:

_____
_____
_____
_____

"The LORD is my strength and my shield; my heart trusts in Him, and He helps me. My heart leaps for joy, and with my song I praise Him." - Psalm 28:7

MY PRAYER REQUEST (INCLUDE THE DATE):

_____

_____

_____

_____

_____

_____

_____

_____

_____

_____

HOW & WHEN GOD RESPONDED TO MY PRAYER:

_____

_____

_____

_____

WHAT THIS EXPERIENCE TAUGHT ME ABOUT GOD:

_____

_____

_____

_____

"For nothing will be impossible with God." - Luke 1:37

MY PRAYER REQUEST (INCLUDE THE DATE):

_____
_____
_____
_____
_____
_____
_____
_____
_____
_____

HOW & WHEN GOD RESPONDED TO MY PRAYER:

_____
_____
_____
_____

WHAT THIS EXPERIENCE TAUGHT ME ABOUT GOD:

_____
_____
_____
_____

"Continue steadfastly in prayer, being watchful in it with thanksgiving."
- Colossians 4:2

MY PRAYER REQUEST (INCLUDE THE DATE):

_____
_____
_____
_____
_____
_____
_____
_____
_____
_____

HOW & WHEN GOD RESPONDED TO MY PRAYER:

_____
_____
_____
_____

WHAT THIS EXPERIENCE TAUGHT ME ABOUT GOD:

_____
_____
_____
_____

"Our ancestors trusted in You, and You rescued them. They cried out to You and were saved. They trusted in You and were never disgraced." - Psalm 22:4-5

MY PRAYER REQUEST (INCLUDE THE DATE):

_____
_____
_____
_____
_____
_____
_____
_____
_____

HOW & WHEN GOD RESPONDED TO MY PRAYER:

_____
_____
_____
_____

WHAT THIS EXPERIENCE TAUGHT ME ABOUT GOD:

_____
_____
_____
_____

"If you remain in me and my words remain in you, ask for whatever you want and it will be done for you." - John 15:7

MY PRAYER REQUEST (INCLUDE THE DATE):

_____
_____
_____
_____
_____
_____
_____
_____
_____
_____

HOW & WHEN GOD RESPONDED TO MY PRAYER:

_____
_____
_____
_____

WHAT THIS EXPERIENCE TAUGHT ME ABOUT GOD:

_____
_____
_____
_____

"He is near to those who call to him, who call to him with sincerity." - Psalm 145:18

MY PRAYER REQUEST (INCLUDE THE DATE):

_____
_____
_____
_____
_____
_____
_____
_____
_____
_____

HOW & WHEN GOD RESPONDED TO MY PRAYER:

_____
_____
_____
_____

WHAT THIS EXPERIENCE TAUGHT ME ABOUT GOD:

_____
_____
_____
_____

"When you call me and come and pray to me, I will listen to you. You will seek me and find me when you search for me with all your heart." - Jeremiah 29:12-13

MY PRAYER REQUEST (INCLUDE THE DATE):

_____
_____
_____
_____
_____
_____
_____
_____
_____
_____

HOW & WHEN GOD RESPONDED TO MY PRAYER:

_____
_____
_____
_____

WHAT THIS EXPERIENCE TAUGHT ME ABOUT GOD:

_____
_____
_____
_____

"For I cried out to him for help, praising him as I spoke. If I had not confessed the sin in my heart, the Lord would not have listened. But God did listen! He paid attention to my prayer. Praise God, who did not ignore my prayer or withdraw his unfailing love from me." - Psalm 66:17-20

MY PRAYER REQUEST(INCLUDE THE DATE):

_____
_____
_____
_____
_____
_____
_____
_____
_____
_____

HOW & WHEN GOD RESPONDED TO MY PRAYER:

_____
_____
_____
_____

WHAT THIS EXPERIENCE TAUGHT ME ABOUT GOD:

_____
_____
_____
_____

"Don't be anxious about anything; rather, bring up all of your requests to God in your prayers and petitions, along with giving thanks." - Philippians 4:6

MY PRAYER REQUEST (INCLUDE THE DATE):

_____
_____
_____
_____
_____
_____
_____
_____
_____
_____

HOW & WHEN GOD RESPONDED TO MY PRAYER:

_____
_____
_____
_____

WHAT THIS EXPERIENCE TAUGHT ME ABOUT GOD:

_____
_____
_____
_____

"Lord, in the morning you hear my voice. In the morning I lay it all out before you. Then I wait expectantly." - Psalm 5:3

MY PRAYER REQUEST(INCLUDE THE DATE):

___

HOW & WHEN GOD RESPONDED TO MY PRAYER:

___

WHAT THIS EXPERIENCE TAUGHT ME ABOUT GOD:

___

"So we fasted and prayed to our God for this, and he responded to us." - Ezra 8:23

MY PRAYER REQUEST (INCLUDE THE DATE):

_____
_____
_____
_____
_____
_____
_____
_____
_____
_____

HOW & WHEN GOD RESPONDED TO MY PRAYER:

_____
_____
_____
_____

WHAT THIS EXPERIENCE TAUGHT ME ABOUT GOD:

_____
_____
_____
_____

"And I tell you: Ask and you will receive. Seek and you will find. Knock and the door will be opened to you." - Luke 11:9

MY PRAYER REQUEST (INCLUDE THE DATE):

___

___

___

___

___

___

___

___

___

HOW & WHEN GOD RESPONDED TO MY PRAYER:

___

___

___

___

WHAT THIS EXPERIENCE TAUGHT ME ABOUT GOD:

___

___

___

___

"You will keep in perfect peace all who trust in You, all whose thoughts are fixed on You! Trust in the Lord always, for the Lord God is the eternal Rock." - Isaiah 26:3-4

MY PRAYER REQUEST(INCLUDE THE DATE):

___

HOW & WHEN GOD RESPONDED TO MY PRAYER:

___

WHAT THIS EXPERIENCE TAUGHT ME ABOUT GOD:

___

"The lions may grow weak and hungry, but those who seek the LORD lack no good thing." - Psalm 34:10

MY PRAYER REQUEST (INCLUDE THE DATE):

_____
_____
_____
_____
_____
_____
_____
_____
_____

HOW & WHEN GOD RESPONDED TO MY PRAYER:

_____
_____
_____
_____

WHAT THIS EXPERIENCE TAUGHT ME ABOUT GOD:

_____
_____
_____
_____

"Let us then approach God's throne of grace with confidence, so that we may receive mercy and find grace to help us in our time of need." - Hebrews 4:16

MY PRAYER REQUEST (INCLUDE THE DATE):

___

HOW & WHEN GOD RESPONDED TO MY PRAYER:

___

WHAT THIS EXPERIENCE TAUGHT ME ABOUT GOD:

___

"If you ask Me for anything in My name, I will do it." - John 14:14

MY PRAYER REQUEST (INCLUDE THE DATE):

_____
_____
_____
_____
_____
_____
_____
_____
_____
_____

HOW & WHEN GOD RESPONDED TO MY PRAYER:

_____
_____
_____
_____

WHAT THIS EXPERIENCE TAUGHT ME ABOUT GOD:

_____
_____
_____
_____

*"Trust in the LORD with all your heart; do not depend on your own understanding.
Seek His will in all you do, and He will show you which path to take."*
- Proverbs 3:5-6

MY PRAYER REQUEST (INCLUDE THE DATE):

_____
_____
_____
_____
_____
_____
_____
_____
_____
_____

HOW & WHEN GOD RESPONDED TO MY PRAYER:

_____
_____
_____
_____

WHAT THIS EXPERIENCE TAUGHT ME ABOUT GOD:

_____
_____
_____
_____

"Give all your worries and cares to God, for He cares about you." - 1 Peter 5:7

MY PRAYER REQUEST (INCLUDE THE DATE):

_____
_____
_____
_____
_____
_____
_____
_____
_____
_____

HOW & WHEN GOD RESPONDED TO MY PRAYER:

_____
_____
_____
_____

WHAT THIS EXPERIENCE TAUGHT ME ABOUT GOD:

_____
_____
_____
_____

"I waited patiently for the LORD to help me, and He turned to me and heard my cry."
- Psalm 40:1

MY PRAYER REQUEST (INCLUDE THE DATE):

_____
_____
_____
_____
_____
_____
_____
_____
_____
_____
_____

HOW & WHEN GOD RESPONDED TO MY PRAYER:

_____
_____
_____
_____

WHAT THIS EXPERIENCE TAUGHT ME ABOUT GOD:

_____
_____
_____
_____

"But blessed is the one who trusts in the LORD, whose confidence is in him."
- Jeremiah 17:7

MY PRAYER REQUEST (INCLUDE THE DATE):

_____
_____
_____
_____
_____
_____
_____
_____
_____
_____

HOW & WHEN GOD RESPONDED TO MY PRAYER:

_____
_____
_____
_____

WHAT THIS EXPERIENCE TAUGHT ME ABOUT GOD:

_____
_____
_____
_____

"Those who know your name trust in you, for you, O LORD, do not abandon those who search for you." - Psalm 9:10

MY PRAYER REQUEST (INCLUDE THE DATE):

_____
_____
_____
_____
_____
_____
_____
_____
_____
_____

HOW & WHEN GOD RESPONDED TO MY PRAYER:

_____
_____
_____
_____

WHAT THIS EXPERIENCE TAUGHT ME ABOUT GOD:

_____
_____
_____
_____

"This is the confidence we have in approaching God: that if we ask anything according to His will, He hears us." - 1 John 5:14

MY PRAYER REQUEST (INCLUDE THE DATE):

_____
_____
_____
_____
_____
_____
_____
_____
_____

HOW & WHEN GOD RESPONDED TO MY PRAYER:

_____
_____
_____
_____

WHAT THIS EXPERIENCE TAUGHT ME ABOUT GOD:

_____
_____
_____
_____

"O my people, trust in Him at all times. Pour out your heart to Him, for God is our refuge." - Psalm 62:8

MY PRAYER REQUEST (INCLUDE THE DATE):

_____
_____
_____
_____
_____
_____
_____
_____
_____
_____

HOW & WHEN GOD RESPONDED TO MY PRAYER:

_____
_____
_____
_____

WHAT THIS EXPERIENCE TAUGHT ME ABOUT GOD:

_____
_____
_____
_____

"Jesus was telling them a parable about their need to pray continuously and not to be discouraged." - Luke 18:1

MY PRAYER REQUEST (INCLUDE THE DATE):

___

HOW & WHEN GOD RESPONDED TO MY PRAYER:

___

WHAT THIS EXPERIENCE TAUGHT ME ABOUT GOD:

___

"And it is impossible to please God without faith. Anyone who wants to come to Him must believe that God exists and that He rewards those who sincerely seek Him."
- Hebrews 11:6

MY PRAYER REQUEST (INCLUDE THE DATE):

_____
_____
_____
_____
_____
_____
_____
_____
_____
_____

HOW & WHEN GOD RESPONDED TO MY PRAYER:

_____
_____
_____
_____

WHAT THIS EXPERIENCE TAUGHT ME ABOUT GOD:

_____
_____
_____
_____

"I call on you, my God, for You will answer me; turn Your ear to me and hear my prayer." - Psalm 17:6

MY PRAYER REQUEST (INCLUDE THE DATE):

_____
_____
_____
_____
_____
_____
_____
_____
_____
_____

HOW & WHEN GOD RESPONDED TO MY PRAYER:

_____
_____
_____
_____

WHAT THIS EXPERIENCE TAUGHT ME ABOUT GOD:

_____
_____
_____
_____

"Pray continually." -1 Thessalonians 5:17

MY PRAYER REQUEST (INCLUDE THE DATE):

_____
_____
_____
_____
_____
_____
_____
_____
_____
_____

HOW & WHEN GOD RESPONDED TO MY PRAYER:

_____
_____
_____
_____

WHAT THIS EXPERIENCE TAUGHT ME ABOUT GOD:

_____
_____
_____
_____

"The LORD is my strength and my shield; my heart trusts in Him, and He helps me. My heart leaps for joy, and with my song I praise Him." - Psalm 28:7

MY PRAYER REQUEST(INCLUDE THE DATE):

_____
_____
_____
_____
_____
_____
_____
_____
_____

HOW & WHEN GOD RESPONDED TO MY PRAYER:

_____
_____
_____
_____

WHAT THIS EXPERIENCE TAUGHT ME ABOUT GOD:

_____
_____
_____
_____

"For nothing will be impossible with God." - Luke 1:37

MY PRAYER REQUEST(INCLUDE THE DATE):

_____
_____
_____
_____
_____
_____
_____
_____
_____

HOW & WHEN GOD RESPONDED TO MY PRAYER:

_____
_____
_____
_____

WHAT THIS EXPERIENCE TAUGHT ME ABOUT GOD:

_____
_____
_____
_____

"Continue steadfastly in prayer, being watchful in it with thanksgiving."
- Colossians 4:2

MY PRAYER REQUEST (INCLUDE THE DATE):

_____
_____
_____
_____
_____
_____
_____
_____

HOW & WHEN GOD RESPONDED TO MY PRAYER:

_____
_____
_____
_____

WHAT THIS EXPERIENCE TAUGHT ME ABOUT GOD:

_____
_____
_____
_____

"Our ancestors trusted in You, and You rescued them. They cried out to You and were saved. They trusted in You and were never disgraced." - Psalm 22:4-5

MY PRAYER REQUEST(INCLUDE THE DATE):

_____
_____
_____
_____
_____
_____
_____
_____
_____

HOW & WHEN GOD RESPONDED TO MY PRAYER:

_____
_____
_____
_____

WHAT THIS EXPERIENCE TAUGHT ME ABOUT GOD:

_____
_____
_____
_____

"If you remain in me and my words remain in you, ask for whatever you want and it will be done for you." - John 15:7

MY PRAYER REQUEST (INCLUDE THE DATE):

_____
_____
_____
_____
_____
_____
_____
_____
_____

HOW & WHEN GOD RESPONDED TO MY PRAYER:

_____
_____
_____
_____

WHAT THIS EXPERIENCE TAUGHT ME ABOUT GOD:

_____
_____
_____
_____

"He is near to those who call to him, who call to him with sincerity." - Psalm 145:18

MY PRAYER REQUEST (INCLUDE THE DATE):

___

HOW & WHEN GOD RESPONDED TO MY PRAYER:

___

WHAT THIS EXPERIENCE TAUGHT ME ABOUT GOD:

___

"When you call me and come and pray to me, I will listen to you. You will seek me and find me when you search for me with all your heart." - Jeremiah 29:12-13

MY PRAYER REQUEST (INCLUDE THE DATE):

_____
_____
_____
_____
_____
_____
_____
_____
_____

HOW & WHEN GOD RESPONDED TO MY PRAYER:

_____
_____
_____
_____

WHAT THIS EXPERIENCE TAUGHT ME ABOUT GOD:

_____
_____
_____
_____

"For I cried out to him for help, praising him as I spoke. If I had not confessed the sin in my heart, the Lord would not have listened. But God did listen! He paid attention to my prayer. Praise God, who did not ignore my prayer or withdraw his unfailing love from me." - Psalm 66:17-20

MY PRAYER REQUEST (INCLUDE THE DATE):

_____
_____
_____
_____
_____
_____
_____
_____
_____
_____

HOW & WHEN GOD RESPONDED TO MY PRAYER:

_____
_____
_____
_____

WHAT THIS EXPERIENCE TAUGHT ME ABOUT GOD:

_____
_____
_____
_____

"Don't be anxious about anything; rather, bring up all of your requests to God in your prayers and petitions, along with giving thanks." - Philippians 4:6

MY PRAYER REQUEST (INCLUDE THE DATE):

_____
_____
_____
_____
_____
_____
_____
_____

HOW & WHEN GOD RESPONDED TO MY PRAYER:

_____
_____
_____
_____

WHAT THIS EXPERIENCE TAUGHT ME ABOUT GOD:

_____
_____
_____
_____

"Lord, in the morning you hear my voice. In the morning I lay it all out before you. Then I wait expectantly." - Psalm 5:3

MY PRAYER REQUEST(INCLUDE THE DATE):

_____
_____
_____
_____
_____
_____
_____
_____
_____
_____

HOW & WHEN GOD RESPONDED TO MY PRAYER:

_____
_____
_____
_____
_____

WHAT THIS EXPERIENCE TAUGHT ME ABOUT GOD:

_____
_____
_____
_____

"So we fasted and prayed to our God for this, and he responded to us." - Ezra 8:23

MY PRAYER REQUEST (INCLUDE THE DATE):

_____
_____
_____
_____
_____
_____
_____
_____
_____

HOW & WHEN GOD RESPONDED TO MY PRAYER:

_____
_____
_____
_____

WHAT THIS EXPERIENCE TAUGHT ME ABOUT GOD:

_____
_____
_____
_____

"And I tell you: Ask and you will receive. Seek and you will find. Knock and the door will be opened to you." - Luke 11:9

MY PRAYER REQUEST (INCLUDE THE DATE):

_____
_____
_____
_____
_____
_____
_____
_____
_____
_____

HOW & WHEN GOD RESPONDED TO MY PRAYER:

_____
_____
_____
_____

WHAT THIS EXPERIENCE TAUGHT ME ABOUT GOD:

_____
_____
_____
_____

"You will keep in perfect peace all who trust in You, all whose thoughts are fixed on You! Trust in the Lord always, for the Lord God is the eternal Rock." - Isaiah 26:3-4

MY PRAYER REQUEST (INCLUDE THE DATE):

_____
_____
_____
_____
_____
_____
_____
_____
_____

HOW & WHEN GOD RESPONDED TO MY PRAYER:

_____
_____
_____
_____

WHAT THIS EXPERIENCE TAUGHT ME ABOUT GOD:

_____
_____
_____
_____

"The lions may grow weak and hungry, but those who seek the LORD lack no good thing." - Psalm 34:10

MY PRAYER REQUEST (INCLUDE THE DATE):

_____
_____
_____
_____
_____
_____
_____
_____
_____

HOW & WHEN GOD RESPONDED TO MY PRAYER:

_____
_____
_____
_____

WHAT THIS EXPERIENCE TAUGHT ME ABOUT GOD:

_____
_____
_____
_____

"Let us then approach God's throne of grace with confidence, so that we may receive mercy and find grace to help us in our time of need." - Hebrews 4:16

MY PRAYER REQUEST (INCLUDE THE DATE):

_____
_____
_____
_____
_____
_____
_____
_____
_____
_____

HOW & WHEN GOD RESPONDED TO MY PRAYER:

_____
_____
_____
_____

WHAT THIS EXPERIENCE TAUGHT ME ABOUT GOD:

_____
_____
_____
_____

"If you ask Me for anything in My name, I will do it." - John 14:14

MY PRAYER REQUEST (INCLUDE THE DATE):

_____
_____
_____
_____
_____
_____
_____
_____
_____
_____

HOW & WHEN GOD RESPONDED TO MY PRAYER:

_____
_____
_____
_____

WHAT THIS EXPERIENCE TAUGHT ME ABOUT GOD:

_____
_____
_____
_____

*"Trust in the LORD with all your heart; do not depend on your own understanding.
Seek His will in all you do, and He will show you which path to take."*
- Proverbs 3:5-6

MY PRAYER REQUEST (INCLUDE THE DATE):

_____
_____
_____
_____
_____
_____
_____
_____
_____

HOW & WHEN GOD RESPONDED TO MY PRAYER:

_____
_____
_____
_____

WHAT THIS EXPERIENCE TAUGHT ME ABOUT GOD:

_____
_____
_____
_____

"Give all your worries and cares to God, for He cares about you." - 1 Peter 5:7

MY PRAYER REQUEST (INCLUDE THE DATE):

_____
_____
_____
_____
_____
_____
_____
_____
_____
_____

HOW & WHEN GOD RESPONDED TO MY PRAYER:

_____
_____
_____
_____

WHAT THIS EXPERIENCE TAUGHT ME ABOUT GOD:

_____
_____
_____
_____

"I waited patiently for the LORD to help me, and He turned to me and heard my cry."
- Psalm 40:1

MY PRAYER REQUEST (INCLUDE THE DATE):

_____
_____
_____
_____
_____
_____
_____
_____
_____

HOW & WHEN GOD RESPONDED TO MY PRAYER:

_____
_____
_____
_____

WHAT THIS EXPERIENCE TAUGHT ME ABOUT GOD:

_____
_____
_____
_____

"But blessed is the one who trusts in the LORD, whose confidence is in him."
- Jeremiah 17:7

MY PRAYER REQUEST (INCLUDE THE DATE):

_____
_____
_____
_____
_____
_____
_____
_____
_____

HOW & WHEN GOD RESPONDED TO MY PRAYER:

_____
_____
_____
_____

WHAT THIS EXPERIENCE TAUGHT ME ABOUT GOD:

_____
_____
_____
_____

"Those who know your name trust in you, for you, O LORD, do not abandon those who search for you." - Psalm 9:10

Made in the USA
Monee, IL
07 June 2025

37fcf48a-e8bb-423d-a91d-7493ed6ab910R01